P9-CQG-998

PAPERCUT THIS BOOK

TECHNIQUES, TEMPLATES, AND PAPER

Boo Paterson

Abrams, New York

Dedicated to the memory of my great friends Ian Ferguson, Jason Lyons,
Fred Terry, and Stewart McNee

Library of Congress Control Number: 2017932366

ISBN: 978-1-4197-2805-1

Text and illustrations copyright © 2017 Boo Paterson
Photographs by Aly Wight

Published in 2017 by Abrams, an imprint of ABRAMS. All rights reserved. No
portion of this book may be reproduced, stored in a retrieval system, or
transmitted in any form or by any means, mechanical, electronic, photocopying,
recording, or otherwise, without written permission from the publisher.

Printed and bound in China
10 9 8 7 6 5 4 3 2 1

Abrams books are available at special discounts when purchased in quantity for
premiums and promotions as well as fundraising or educational use.
Special editions can also be created to specification.
For details, contact specialsales@abramsbooks.com or the address below.

ABRAMS The Art of Books
115 West 18th Street, New York, NY 10011
abramsbooks.com

CONTENTS

INTRODUCTION

Papercutting is a slow art, which is why it's so relaxing to do. Because it requires a lot of concentration, I find that hours can go by unnoticed—exactly as they did when I was absorbed by creative tasks as a child. I began making things out of paper when I was three or four, and have a very clear memory from that time of creating a birdcage out of yellow printer paper, liberally doused in glitter. My love for the colors, texture, and flexibility of paper never waned and I went on to make pop-up toy theatres, papier mâché sculptures, and papercut artworks.

I've structured this book so that the templates are arranged in order of difficulty—from the easiest to the hardest. It is best to start at the beginning and work your way through, so you can practice papercutting and develop your own technique.

I would suggest using the cream paper supplied in this book for the papercut, and mounting it onto the colored paper. If you'd prefer to use colored paper for the cutting, try brands such as Fabriano Tiziano, Daler Rowney Murano, or Canson Mi-Teintes for the best result.

All papercutting artists make mistakes from time to time, so don't feel you've ruined the artwork if you cut off a vital bit. Mistakes can usually be remedied, as I explain in the instructions.

I use at least one new blade per picture, but there are no set rules—change them more often if you feel it's easier. Everyone has a different hand pressure, and you will learn what's best as you become more masterful at papercutting.

Take your time, and don't feel the need to complete a papercut all in one go—it should be a pleasure to work on something so intricate and delicate, not a mad rush. Most of all, enjoy the process as much as the result, and try to relax into the childlike absorption of the creative process.

4

HOW TO PAPERCUT

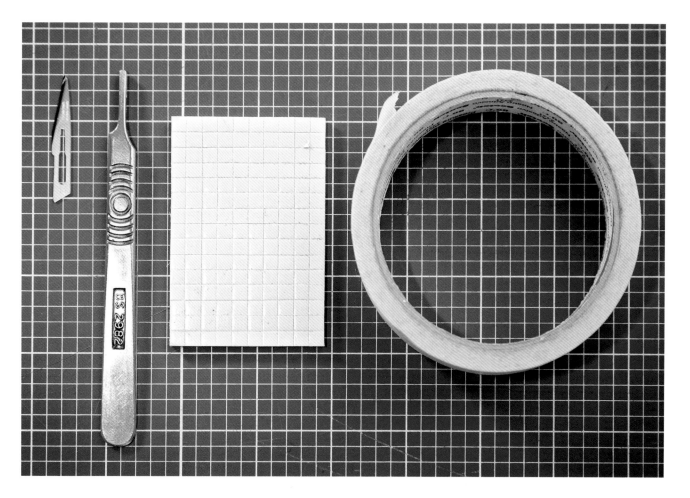

TOOLS

To complete the papercut projects in this book, you will need:

24 x 36-inch cutting mat

1 pack of 20 No. 11 scalpel blades *
(sterile or non-sterile)

1 No. 3 scalpel *(It is recommended that left-handed people choose left-handed scalpels.)

Adhesive foam squares

1 roll masking tape

Needle-nose pliers (not shown)

* Publisher's note: alternative cutting tools are available and you may wish to use the cutting tool of your choice; however, Boo would always advise working with a scalpel blade.

All these items are readily available from most art stores.

SAFELY USING THE SCALPEL

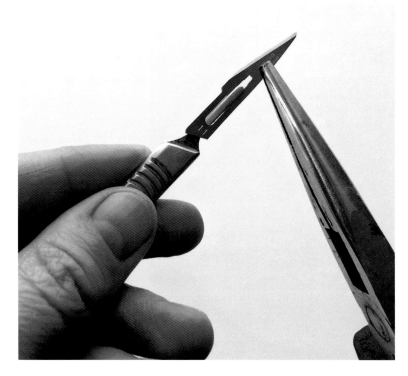

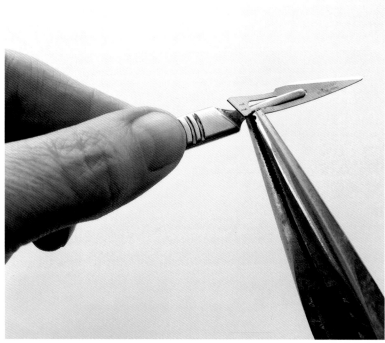

TO LOAD A BLADE

Tear open the metal blade packet in the direction of the arrows, and you will see five paper packets. Remove one, and carefully unfold the paper packet.

Drop the blade onto your mat, and use needle-nose pliers to grasp the back of the blade, with the sharp side facing away from you. Insert the blade into the slot in the scalpel handle. The blade should snap in easily and feel very secure once loaded.

For safety, remove the blade before storing the scalpel, or store your loaded scalpel in a metal pencil case. Alternatively, slice a wine cork halfway through lengthwise with a utility knife, and place your scalpel blade sharp-side in.

TO REMOVE A BLADE

Grasp the blade with the pliers along the back of the blade, and make sure the blade is facing away from you and slightly downward (toward your cutting mat) when removing it.

Lift the blade slightly with the pliers and slide off away from you. Place the used blade in a screw-top glass jar. Once this is full, contact your local garbage collection service for information on where to dispose of sharps safely.

It is also possible to buy blade removers, which not only remove the blade but seal it for disposal. For more information, check the manufacturer's instructions and see my video at boopaterson.com

PREPARING TO CUT

1 Sit at a sturdy table that does not move when you exert downward pressure on it. Place your cutting mat so your hands are comfortably in the middle of it when you are seated.

Detach a sheet of paper from the book, by tearing down the perforated line, and place it on the mat. Tape it down so that only a thin edge of tape covers the paper. Make sure to smooth any air out from under the sheet as you tape the last edge, so it is completely flat and doesn't have any unevenness across the surface.

2 Next, choose the template of the papercut you'd like to create and detach the template from the book. I have placed the templates in order of difficulty—with the easiest at the beginning—so you can build up your technique as you work through. Align the template directly over the paper and tape across the top to hold it in place.

3 Tape the template down securely around the remaining sides—leaving a narrow gap between any blacked-out areas and the edge of the tape. Again, be sure to smooth out any air pockets before taping the last edge down.

CUTTING

1 Hold the knife almost as you would a pen. Your index finger can sit on the long support *behind* the blade, but never *on* the blade itself.

Always cut toward yourself, turning the board so that you are cutting downward each time, and keep your free hand above, or to the side of the cut that you're making, steadying the paper.

2 The general rule is to start in the middle and work your way outward, leaving the straight outer lines until last. Cut the smallest details first, as the more the cut progresses the more unstable the paper becomes, and the harder it is to cut small things without the paper moving around.

To remove tiny areas—such as the parrot's eye—it is best to press the tip of the blade in four times around to make a little square, and then smooth out the edges into a circle when the template is removed.

3 Cut slowly, with an even pressure. With a new blade, you will need very little pressure to cut through both pieces of paper, but as the cut goes on and the blade becomes blunt, you will need to apply more. With some of the very intricate templates near the end of the book, you may require two or three blades per cut.

When you have completed the small details, cut down the black lines next.

4 The dotted lines are to be scored with the back of the blade. They are best done near the beginning of the cut, as with the smaller areas.

5 Cut out all the blacked-out areas next. It is not necessary to cut tight curves or circles all in one go—you can do these as a succession of little cuts, turning the board as you go.

I have found it best not to use a ruler for the straight lines—once in the paper your blade will not waver, and it is easy enough to drag it in a straight line.

FINISHED TEMPLATE

1   When you have cut all the black areas and scored the dotted lines, carefully pull up the tape holding the template down at one corner, and then slowly peel the template back.

2   On the papercut beneath you will see that most of the cut-out areas are still in place.

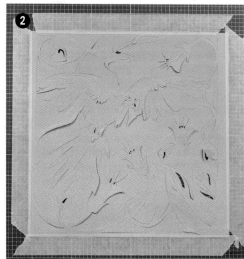

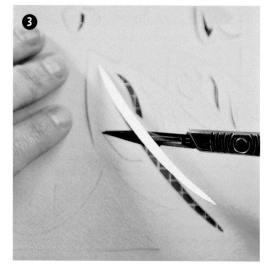

3 Use your scalpel to lift these loose pieces. You can also use your blade to tidy up any rough edges.

Steady the cut while your free hand lifts the paper, and use the blade to go over any areas—such as sharp corners—that are not cut all the way through

4 When your completed papercut has had all the blanks removed, detach the tape holding down the paper by slowly pulling it back over itself—don't pull upward, as this can tear the paper.

REPAIRS

If you've made a mistake by slicing through an area that should have been left in one piece, you can now repair this. Tape a piece of masking tape, roughly the same length and width as the area to be fixed, to your board with the sticky side facing down. Cut out a sliver of it as a "Band-Aid" and lift off the board with the tip of your blade. This can be placed on the back of the papercut to join the two pieces back together invisibly.

CREATING BAS-RELIEF

1 First, make sure your hands are clean and free of grease. Using the photo of the finished work as a guide, manipulate the paper over your fingers to get more of a 3-D look. Bend some areas gently into a curve.

2 Push other areas slightly backward.

3 Gently pull some sections farther forward.

4 Make a fold in smaller pieces to give them some shape.

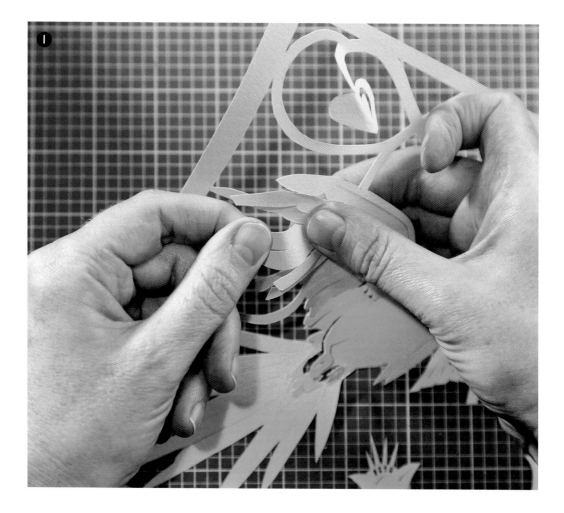

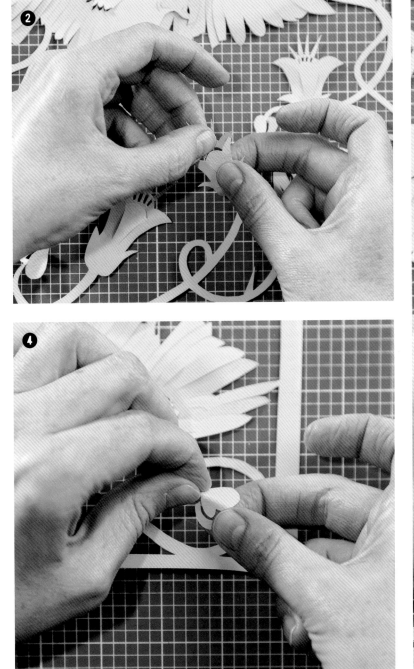

MOUNTING YOUR WORK

1 Turn the papercut over so the back is facing upward. Place the adhesive foam squares at regular intervals around the edge, cutting them in half with your blade wherever narrower ones are needed.

2 Place more foam squares at places where the work needs to be lifted or supported, such as at the base of flower stems.

3 Once the foam squares are set, remove the paper backing from each one and carefully position the papercut over your chosen background color.

4 Your work is now ready to frame. For best results, use a float mount in a box frame.

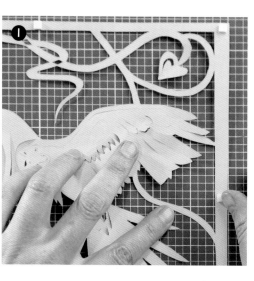

TIGER (P.26)

THE GALLERY

HUMMINGBIRD (P.28)

SLOTH (P.30)

GIRAFFE (P.36)

ORANGUTAN (P.34)

FROG (P.32)

TOUCAN (P.38) LIZARD (P.40)

KANGAROOS (P.44)

BUTTERFLIES (P.46)

22

SUGAR GLIDERS (P.48)

LEMURS (P.50)

PARROT (P.52)

FISH (P.54

24

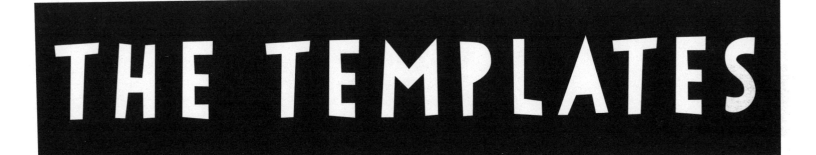

THE TEMPLATES

TIGER

HUMMINGBIRD

SLOTH

FROG

ORANGUTAN

GIRAFFE

TOUCAN

LIZARD

ELEPHANTS

KANGAROOS

BUTTERFLIES

SUGAR GLIDERS

LEMURS

PARROT

FISH